LIFE APPLICABLE LESSONS FROM THE BOOK OF RUTH

Life Applicable Lessons from the Book of Ruth

AN EXPOSITORY ADVENTURE

Anthony Adefarakan

GLOEM, CANADA

Contents

Introduction	1
Part 1	
	3
Lesson #1	5
Lesson #2	7
Lesson #3	9
Lesson #4	11
Lesson #5	13
Lesson #6	15
Part 2	
	17
Lesson #1	19
Lesson #2	21
Lesson #3	23
Lesson #4	25
Lesson #5	27
Lesson #6	29

Part 3

31

Lesson #1 33

Lesson #2 35

Lesson #3 37

Part 4

39

Lesson #1 41

Become a Financial Partner with Jesus 43

About the Author 45

Introduction

Deuteronomy 29:29 says *"the secret things belong unto the LORD our God: but those things which are revealed belong unto us and to our children for ever, that we may do all the words of this law"*

In the journey of life, there are many issues demanding attention; but due to the limited nature of man, several of such issues remain unattended to. Man is limited in scope, vision, knowledge and power; and as a result, he sometimes helplessly watches things go wrong.

However, for a child of God, the case is different. He has access to the secret counsels of the Creator of all things through His Word and His Spirit, thereby drawing on a power greater than his to scale through life victoriously. Such secrets of the Almighty form the content of this book.

Beyond what you already know about the Book of Ruth, the Holy Spirit wishes to show you more lessons capable of helping you live wisely while your sojourn on this planet lasts. Prayerfully read and apply the lessons, you will be blessed beyond measures. You are also free to get copies for or teach others around you, thereby becoming a channel of blessing to your generation. Take this prayer as we embark on an expository adventure into the Book of Ruth.

*"**Open thou mine eyes, that I may behold wondrous things out of thy law**"* –Psalm 119:18

Part 1

LIFE APPLICABLE LESSONS FROM CHAPTER ONE

Lesson #1

As a man, you must learn to take responsibility for your family. Elimelech discovered there was famine in the land which threatened the continued existence of his family. He didn't just sit down in despair; he took a drastic action by finding out where there was food and relocating his family there for sustenance. That's being a responsible husband and father.

Also, we noticed that Naomi, his wife, didn't come up with a contrary vision. She simply complied with her head's instruction and gravitated towards his direction. It was the duty of the man to provide direction for the family and as a responsible wife, she cooperated with her husband. As a result of this demonstration of unity of purpose, their children –Mahlon and Chilion - had no option than to follow suit. When the father plays his role and the mother supports without rebelling, their children will definitely be cooperative. For instance, if the father declares the God of Israel as the God his family will worship and his wife complies, the children will not follow Baal. However, the man must take the lead before expecting his family to follow. He must have a vision for the family which his wife and children are to pursue with him.

It is also worthy of note that the Bible calls Christ the Head of the man (1 Corinthians 11:3). It therefore follows that a man who will provide good direction for his family must be subject to Christ Himself. Following a man who is not under the control of Christ is risky. As a husband, submit to Christ and He will help you lead your family aright.

Your family needs you to point in the way they are to go. So, stand up and take responsibility for your family.

Reference: Ruth 1: 1-2.

Lesson #2

Bad times also happen to God's people. Famine – an extreme scarcity of food – visited God's own people. In Bethlehem, a place known and named as 'the house of bread', there was no bread. Despite being connected to Judah –which means 'praise', their condition was not praiseworthy but life-threatening. There is no level of relationship with God that will keep certain unfavourable situations like famine away permanently. It was recorded in Gen 12:10 that there was a famine in the time of Abraham (despite his close relationship with God), and another one in the time of his son Isaac (Gen 26:1). Their faithful and covenant walk with God couldn't prevent famine from coming. However, according to 1Corinthians 10:13, He had always made a way out for His own. In Gen 41:29-36 for instance, God warned Egypt of an imminent famine through the dream He gave to Pharaoh. He thereafter gave Joseph the wisdom to apply in order to scale through the famine without being hurt by it. It simply follows that though bad times (famine) are inevitable as long as this earth exists, they can be wisely planned for in order to come out of them victoriously.

Reference: Ruth 1:1.

Lesson #3

No condition is permanent. Even if there is famine today, God will visit you with bread once again as recorded in Ruth 1: 6. According to Ecclesiastes 3: 1-8, there is a time for everything under the heavens. If you are in your season of famine now, be very confident that it will soon give way to your season of plenty. Conversely, if you are at present enjoying abundance; be assured that a time of scarcity is also coming. So you must plan to welcome it when it comes.

With this knowledge, it becomes imperative that whenever there is a supply, a certain portion of it is to be set aside in order to scale through the inevitable famine seasons that come to every man on earth. On every income, a portion is to be set aside to ensure sustenance when famine sets in. For every provision the Lord brings your way, He has your survival in the time of famine in mind; and as a result, he expects you to plan for it.

Every season of life should be treated with utmost wisdom. Plenty is not permanent, so you must invest; and famine is not permanent, so you must be courageous to scale through while it lasts. In the case of Egypt, the famine lasted only seven (7) years –Gen 41:29-36, while in the case of Judah, Naomi heard after about ten (10) years that the famine had ended. No famine is eternal as far as this earth is concerned.

Reference: Ruth 1:6.

Lesson #4

Regardless of the kinds of blow the world has dealt or is at present dealing you, never sit down in defeat. Arise and head towards a new beginning. Attempt a fresh start. Acknowledge your unfortunate situation, don't deny it; but never accept it as the conclusion of your condition. In verse 6 of Ruth chapter 1, despite all the woes that had befallen Naomi, she arose and headed for a new beginning. Even if you have fallen up to seven times, God expects you to get up and keep going - Proverbs 24:10, 16.

As a student, you might have failed woefully in times past and may even be planning to give up thinking there is no point trying again. It is too early to quit. You are expected to go at it again. There is always light at the end of the tunnel provided you endure till you get to the end of the tunnel. You must never allow the devil to have the final say or have the last laugh over your life. Rise again, you are more than conquerors.

Reference: Ruth 1:6.

Lesson #5

Tenacity (perseverance) is a vital ingredient for destiny fulfillment. This virtue played out in Ruth 1: 14-18 as Ruth refused to be persuaded against her destiny. She saw something in Naomi's family which was totally different from what her background portrayed and she decided to cling unto that. All effort to derail her was abortive as she tenaciously held on to her resolution. Her sister in law decided to yield after a little persuasion but not Ruth. She was willing to die for what she believed in and according to Matthew 1:5, her tenacity was rewarded as she found herself named among those Jesus Christ, the King of kings descended from. Jacob also exhibited this kind of tenacity in Gen 32:26 and he had his destiny transformed forever.

What is that vision in your heart? You need tenacity to fulfil it. No vision gets fulfilled on a platter of gold; there must be oppositions. It is the ability to overcome these oppositions that guarantees the eventual fulfillment of your dreams. These oppositions may come in form of wrong counsels from friends, undue pressure from family members, death of a loved one, unfavourable economic climate, sickness, disappointments, natural disasters etc. Regardless of the form these oppositions may take, rising above them is the only guarantee that you will have your desires fulfilled. The grace you need to be tenacious until your dreams come to pass, receive it in Jesus' Name.

Reference: Ruth 1: 14-18.

Lesson #6

Never blame your circumstances on God. God is always good. Elimelech died, Mahlon and Chilion also died, leaving Naomi alone. Yet she didn't see the fact that she was the only survivor as God's goodness. She was so clouded with her challenges that she described her condition as God's Hand afflicting her. She attributed all her woes to God being against her – Ruth 1: 19-22. God is the One to run to in times of trouble, not the One to blame. He is good to all (Psalm 145:9, Matthew 5:45). Your condition or circumstances shouldn't paint God as bad. There is nothing bad about God. Instead of focusing on your woes, look for the good Hand of God in all your circumstances. No one has ever received deliverance by blaming or accusing God. Blaming God only keeps you in perpetual defeat. Thank Him even in your pains because that is His will for you in Christ Jesus (1Thess 5:18).

Reference: Ruth 1:19-22.

Prayer Point: Father, you are the One who raised Ruth to help Naomi in her helpless state, please raise loyal helpers for me too. Helpers who will not stop helping me no matter what, raise them for me now in Jesus' Name.

Part 2

LIFE APPLICABLE LESSONS FROM CHAPTER TWO

Lesson #1

Regardless of your mighty connections within and outside your family, until God decides to help you, you won't be helped – Ruth 2:1, 20.

Elimelech had a kinsman described as **a mighty man of wealth**, yet he was so affected by the famine in the land that he had to relocate his nuclear family to Moab. Benefitting from the wealth of Boaz could have cushioned the effect on him but he wasn't a partaker at the time. In 2Kings 6: 26-27, the king of Israel said *'...if the Lord do not help thee, whence shall I help thee...?* By implication, it means your uncle's prosperity or your friend's connection with the highly placed may not be the cure to your unemployment or poverty. You may be surrounded by helpers, I mean those with the solution to your problems; but until the Lord moves them to help you, your struggle continues. God can even use strangers to help you like He raised Ruth, a Moabitess, to help Naomi – Ruth 2:2. Get this once and for all, **only God can help you** (Psalm 121:1-2).

Reference: Ruth 2: 1, 20.

Lesson #2

Action precedes favour. You must do what you can before God will do what you can't – Ruth 2:2-3.

It has been said that the faith that expects God to do everything is an irresponsible faith. God expects you to make efforts before backing you up; He doesn't work with zero efforts. Before He killed Goliath, He needed David to engage the sling (1 Samuel 17); before He parted the Red Sea, He needed Moses to engage the rod (Exodus 14); before He delivered the nations into the hands of Israel, He needed Joshua to engage the sword (Joshua 10); before He collapsed the wall of Jericho, He needed the Israelites to give a shout (Joshua 6); before sending the Messiah, He needed Mary to keep her virginity (Luke 1); and before showing Ruth and Naomi favour through Boaz, He needed Ruth to get out of the house and go out to glean (Ruth 2:2-3). Boaz didn't come to their house, they met on the field. So, if Ruth had remained in the house, she might have missed that God ordained favour.

You need a job, but you won't go out to search; all you do is complain. Even if there is favour waiting for you somewhere, your sitting down at home will rob you of it.

Always do what your strength can still do, and you will see God doing what your strength cannot carry. At that time, you will experience His favour.

Reference: Ruth 2:2-3.

Lesson #3

According to Ruth 2:4, how many employers attract "God bless you" from their employees? That is something every employer must think about. Boaz's servants blessed him. The way you are treating your employees, can they really bless you? Also, as employees, do you see your work as a blessing from God? Hope you are aware that many are jobless? Such thinking should make you overflow with gratitude to your employer. Boaz blessed these servants by engaging them in his harvest, thereby qualifying them for some income. And upon his arrival to check what they were doing, they greeted him by saying **"The Lord bless thee"**.

Reference: Ruth 2:4.

Lesson #4

You reap what you sow – Ruth 2:10. Ruth showed favour to Naomi, a stranger, in Moab; and she reaped favour as a stranger in Israel. What goes round still comes round. Treat others the way you want to be treated so that your harvest will not fill your mouth with bitter pills (Matthew 7:12).

Reference: Ruth 2:10.

Lesson #5

When you appreciate little kindness, you get greater kindness. In verses 8-10, Ruth appreciated the kindness Boaz showed her, and by the time we got to verses 14-17, we saw her enjoying greater favour. Take note of this as well, your attitude is being noticed whether you are aware or not. Somehow, some unseen eyes of men are watching your attitude (verses 11-12); so you can't really hide your attitude.

Reference: Ruth 2:8-10; 14-17.

Lesson #6

Favour may sometimes mean more work. To appreciate the source of the favour therefore, you must be willing to engage the favour through hardwork. According to verses 15-17 of chapter 2, Ruth was favoured by being given more stuff to glean which she diligently did until the evening. God may open a door for you as a favour, but you must be ready to walk through the door and fully explore the opportunity. And that means more work is needed. So, if you are not ready for hardwork, stop praying for God's favour.

Reference: Ruth 2: 15-17.

Prayer Point: Father, you are the One who raised Ruth to help Naomi in her helpless state, please raise loyal helpers for me too. Helpers who will not stop helping me no matter what, raise them for me now in Jesus' Name.

Part 3

LIFE APPLICABLE LESSONS FROM CHAPTER THREE

Lesson #1

Benefitting from the ministry of your helpers.

Naomi gave specific instructions to Ruth in verse 3 capable of establishing her destiny. But then, Ruth needed to cooperate with her helper's instructions in order to derive the associated benefits.

Esther was privileged to receive instructions from her helpers as well [Mordecai and Hegai] according to Esther 2:10, 15-17, 20. She cooperated with their instructions and she attained greatness.

In this dispensation, the Holy Spirit is our Helper and He sometimes passes instructions to us directly while at other times, He uses others to instruct us. Our responsibility as one in need of help is to simply comply with the instructions given. That is the only way if we are to benefit from the ministry of our Helpers.

Reference: Ruth 3:3, Esther 2: 10-20.

Lesson #2

Prepare yourself for Favour.

The very first thing Naomi told Ruth in that verse 3 was "wash thyself". To wash means to remove dirt or other unwanted materials. This can be likened to "shaving" according to Genesis 41:14, when Joseph was to prepare to meet with Pharaoh.

To be properly positioned for divine favour, things like sinful attitudes, old and unpleasant memories, stereotypes and every limiting mentality must be washed away. What happens when washing is done is that one becomes clean.

Then she said, "anoint thineself" – meaning, 'apply' (skills, wisdom etc) and dress in your best robe – showing the importance of appearance (clothes). A man planning to attract favour should not be wearing garments of pity. In Genesis 41:14, Joseph didn't appear before Pharaoh in his prison clothes; he had a change of garment. In the case of Esther, she engaged in purification (Esther 2:9) and before she could approach the King for favour, she had to put on her royal robe (Esther 5:1-2, 4).

If you truly desire God's favour, prepare yourself for it.

Reference: Ruth 3:3, Esther 2:9, Genesis 41:14.

Lesson #3

Be sensitive to Proper Timing.

Naomi told Ruth the time to operate for good results (Ruth 3:3, 7). Not all times are appropriate for certain actions. Being sensitive to proper timing is what yields expected results.

Also in Esther 5:4; 7:1-2 and Genesis 41:33-40, Esther and Joseph worked with proper timing respectively and they experienced greatness. There is a time for everything; you must be sensitive not to be waiting when you are expected to strike.

Reference: Ruth 3:3, 7.

Prayer Point: Father, please at every junction of my life, station destiny helpers to help me succeed in Jesus' Name.

Part 4

LIFE APPLICABLE LESSON FROM CHAPTER FOUR

Lesson #1

All is well that ends well.

The entire Chapter 4 of the Book of Ruth simulates what God does in the realm of the Spirit (unknown to us) between the time we obey His instructions and the time we actually receive our testimonies (results of our obedience).

While studying this chapter, I discovered a divine order of answered prayers for God's children.

This is the order;

1. You receive instructions
2. You cooperate with the instructions by carrying them out
3. You wait in joyful expectation (hope)
4. You then receive your testimony (what you've been expecting).

In other words, discover what to do (via the Word of God especially), do it, wait patiently (in hope and not in anxiety), then receive your testimonies.

God only moves between steps 3 and 4 without your input. That's why it is said that 'while you are waiting, God is working'.

After Ruth had carried out all the instructions Naomi gave her, she reported back to her. Upon hearing that she had done all, Naomi told her to wait and expect her results (Ruth 3:18).

By the time we got to verses 13-17 of Ruth chapter 4, both Naomi and Ruth were already singing a new song. Their story had changed completely and the result of Ruth's obedience had fully matured. The joyful end of this Book is what informs the opening statement in this lesson: "ALL IS WELL THAT ENDS WELL".

Reference: Ruth 4:1-17.

Prayer Point: Father, for every matter that has brought me tears, pain and sorrow, please turn them to testimonies for me in the Name of Jesus. Let all be well with me.

Become a Financial Partner with Jesus

At *Global Emancipation Ministries - Calgary*, our mandate is *to liberate men through the knowledge of the Truth* and our mission statement is *creating channels through which men can encounter the Truth* [Isaiah 61:1-3; John 8:32, 36; I Thessalonians 5:24]

Our Ministerial Activities include Rural and Urban Evangelical Outreaches, Prison Evangelism, Hospital Ministrations, Mobilization for Missions Support, Teaching of the undiluted Word of God, Scripture-Based Seminars, Discipleship, Training of Field Missionaries and Empowerment of underprivileged ones among other Field Ministerial Tasks.

If you sense the Lord is calling you to reach out to the lost by engaging in any of these activities or by assisting those involved with your resources, please feel free to join us. Let us come together as we take the Gospel of our Lord Jesus Christ to the hurting and forgotten ones.

[Mark 16:15-20].

Please join us in these kingdom projects by making your weekly, monthly, quarterly or annual donations to Global Emancipation Ministries – Calgary.

You can visit the "GIVE" section on our website, www.gloem.org, to learn about ways to give.

For acknowledgement, please advise your donations to us by email: info@gloem.org or emancipation4souls@yahoo.com, and kindly include your details i.e. name, address, email and location. Alternatively, you can simply call +1 587 9735910 to do same.

You can also volunteer your gifts and talents in the service of the Lord through our ministerial platforms regardless of your location. To get information on how to go about this, please visit www.gloem.org and contact us via email: info@gloem.org or emancipation4souls@yahoo.com.

God bless you.

About the Author

By the special grace of God, **Anthony O. Adefarakan** is the privileged President of **Global Emancipation Ministries - Calgary (GLOEM)** with headquarters in Canada, North America and **Emancipating Truth Ministry International (ETMI)** with headquarters in Nigeria, West Africa.

The Lord called him into the field ministry in February 2008 with the mandate to liberate men through the knowledge of the Truth, and by December 2012 he was ordained and commissioned as the Pioneer Pastor – in – Charge of The Redeemed Christian Church of God, Revelation Parish, Shalom Area under Delta Province III, Nigeria where he served until 1st February 2015 when he officially handed over to a new Pastor in order to focus on his field ministry to which the Lord had earlier called him and for which the authority of the church had already prayed and released him to undertake.

On 29th September 2013, he was awarded a Post Graduate Diploma in Tent – Making Mission from the Redeemed Christian School of Missions, Nigeria (RECSOM, Asaba Campus) where he also had the privilege to train Pastors and Missionaries as a lecturer in 2017.

Since the commissioning of his field ministry in 2015 he has had the opportunity to lead his ministry officers to field ministrations in different Prisons, Hospitals, Orphanages, Rural communities, Camp settlements, Markets, Local churches among other places with great successes on all occasions – such as salvation of sinners, healing of the sick, financial empowerment of mission churches, provision of relief materials to the poor, provision of medical services to the underprivileged, baptism in the Holy Ghost, deliverance from demonic oppression, release of inmates just to mention a few - all to the glory of God Who alone is the Doer.

He is the author of other best-selling titles such as ***Learning from the Ants, It's Your Size, The Immutability of God's Counsel, Surely there is an End, Life Applicable lessons from the Book of Ruth, The Law of Kinds, One thing is Needful , Life Applicable Revelations from God's Word*** among others.

He is happily married to Ifeoluwa A. Adefarakan and their marriage is fruitful to the glory of God.

Jesus is his Message, Freedom is the Outcome!

Isaiah 61:1-3

www.ingramcontent.com/pod-product-compliance
Lightning Source LLC
Chambersburg PA
CBHW062205100526
44589CB00014B/1959